Millionaire Success Manual

Wealth Habits and Money Making Methods

Table of Contents

Introduction

Chapter 1: Creating a Millionaire

Chapter 2: Millionaire Mindset

Chapter 3: Habits of Millionaires and Billionaires

Chapter 4: You Must Be Better Than Everyone

Chapter 5: Types of Income

Chapter 6: Take Advantage of the Internet

Chapter 7: The Power of Your Team

Chapter 8: Take The Pledge

Conclusion

Introduction

Not a single millionaire came into their financial wealth without a solid plan. Short of winning the lottery, there is no way to generate massive amounts of wealth without a clear plan on how you are going to do it. Even then, if you want to be a *successful* millionaire, you have to have a plan. People who come into massive amounts of wealth without a plan always end up losing their money within' a few years' time. Learning to be a successful millionaire comes from learning to discipline yourself, set goals and work towards them, and persevere even when times are hard. If you want to be a successful millionaire, you need to learn to master the various areas of your life that are congruent with the true millionaire lifestyle - not just the one you see on TV.

"*Millionaire Success Manual*: Wealth Habits and Money Making Methods" emphasizes on what differentiates a millionaire from a non-millionaire and how you can achieve millionaire status in your own life. It is crucial that you understand that only 1% of the entire population will achieve millionaire status. If you want to achieve this status, you must dedicate yourself to the process. While you will take a proper millionaire pledge at the end of this book, you should start right now by taking a smaller pledge. Repeat the following sentence out loud three times: "I, (your name), will read this book from cover to cover so that I can understand what it takes to become a millionaire." If you can commit to reading this book, then you will be given all of the tools that you need in order to achieve millionaire status in your life.

This book was written from a millionaire mentality, so you can be certain that everything within' these pages will direct you towards being a millionaire. If you follow the steps and take the time to educate yourself on each process, you will have all of the tools that you need to achieve a millionaire lifestyle. However, in order to do so you must read each chapter so that you can gain the valuable knowledge from this book. Now that you have taken the pledge and are committed to achieving success, you can dive into the chapters. Please take your time and make sure that you truly let each piece of information absorb into your mind so that you can successfully absorb all that you need to know in order to become a millionaire. Also, enjoy.

Chapter 1: Creating a Millionaire

"Before you can become a millionaire, you must learn to think like one. You must learn how to motivate yourself to counter fear with courage. Making critical decisions about your career, business, investments and other resources conjures up fear, fear that is part of the process of becoming a financial success."

- *Thomas J. Stanley*

From a poor person's perspective there is only one thing that goes into creating a millionaire: money. People who do not have money believe that the only thing that is required to make a person wealthy is money. While money is what creates the definition of wealthy, it certainly isn't the only element required in actually making a millionaire. If you want to become a millionaire, you must learn all of the steps that actually go into becoming one.

Emphasize On What You Need to Know

Education is a pain point for many people who are seeking to become a millionaire. They either sink tens of thousands of dollars into an educational degree that only serves them in one way, or they complain that they don't have enough education to make money. The reality is that a large majority of the people who are millionaires are not educated about their businesses through an actual education or university degree.

In fact, the smartest millionaires are those who chose the field they wanted to get into and then invested their time learning what they needed to know in order to succeed. Those who spend large amounts of time and money gaining more information than they'll ever require to succeed will struggle to succeed in the long run. Massive amounts of debt can lead to financial inadequacy and sometimes being over educated can lead to a whole new realm of problems, such as feeling entitled. While this is not always the case and there are many graduates who will achieve success, it is important that you don't emphasize on your success entirely on what you have learned. Instead, pay attention to what you know about the industry you are getting into and emphasize on that.

When you spend too much time learning about every single thing under a specific industry, you waste valuable time that could have been spent learning about what actually matters. The reality is that only a certain amount of knowledge is required for you to get through the steps and get to where you need to go. Emphasize on what you do know, and make sure that you invest your time in learning what is actually necessary instead of trying to learn every single thing about any given topic.

Be Willing to Sacrifice

No millionaire ever achieved their status by sitting around playing video games or partying every day. If you want to become a millionaire you need to be willing to make sacrifices. People who are not willing to sacrifice their leisure time in favor of making money are not going to become millionaires. While it is important to have leisure time and enjoy your life, it is also important that you spend a significant amount of time invested in creating your financial wealth.

Smart millionaires are ones who schedule time for fun and engage in nothing but fun during that time. They shut off their phones, tune out distractions, and completely invest in the activity they are engaging in. When they do this, they give themselves the opportunity to let loose and enjoy life itself. That way when they are done they can return their entire focus to their goals and continue working towards the money. Even when you are having fun, you need to be mindful of what you are doing. You never want to start spending too much money on your fun as you will end up depleting your savings and you will never become a millionaire.

When it comes to actually getting things done, you need to be willing to make sacrifices to stay focused. The process of becoming a millionaire can become lonely. While all of your friends are out purchasing brand new thing, partying, and doing other entertaining things you are going to need to be focused on earning your wealth. If you can do that, then you are certain to be able to achieve millionaire status.

Accept Defeat and Mistakes

Millionaires know how to accept defeat and mistakes. They can recognize when something was done wrong or hasn't gone their way and they can accept it. Because of their ability to accept it they can move on and use it as a lesson to leverage them into greater success going forward. A millionaire never dwells on defeat or mistakes that they have experienced in their lifetime, regardless of the magnitude.

Learning to let go of mistakes and defeats is a mandatory part of being able to have a millionaire mindset. If you want to achieve millionaire status in your lifetime you need to accept the fact that you are going to endure many instances of defeat and mistakes. The reality is that there is simply no way for you to become a millionaire without making mistakes and being defeat at some points. Being a millionaire means being able to adapt with life and make decisions based on what happens to you and around you. If you make a mistake or are defeat in anyway, you need to accept it, recognize the current situation, and make the necessary changes so that you can continue working towards your success.

Aim Higher

If you want to achieve millionaire status you need to aim higher than a million. Your overall goal should be to make one million, and your long-term goal should be to make much more. Millionaires recognize the importance of their goals and they work towards achieving those goals on a constant basis. Millionaires don't only set realistic goals, they set massive goals. The more you set out to achieve, the harder you are going to work to achieve that.

When you are setting the goal to be a millionaire, set the goal to be a multi-millionaire. That way, you can have something massive to work towards. Also, once you achieve your first million you will be prepared to work harder to achieve your second, third, fourth, fifth and all subsequent millions. Always set your goals substantially higher than you originally set out to achieve, knowing that the bigger you dream, the more you achieve.

Be Honest

A millionaire who makes a million dollars by being a liar is a millionaire who will never maintain his status. Once your reputation is tarnished, no one will invest in you. You will not be able to get partners, no one will want to invest in your products, services, or company, and you will not be able to earn massive income levels. You must understand that one major dent into your reputation can damage your reputation for life. Companies who are exposed for being dishonest can never regain their reputation, even if they completely clear it and work towards the betterment of their reputation for the rest of their days in business.

Your reputation is vital in your ability to become a millionaire. You must learn the importance of your reputation and maintain it by being honest and staying true to your word. A millionaire who stays true to their word is a millionaire who will be able to maintain their status and expand their income even more rapidly than before.

Stop Limiting Yourself

People can limit themselves in an infinite number of ways. Poor mindset, poor habits, and a lack of personal development can all lead to you limiting your ability to achieve success. If you want to become a millionaire the best thing you can do is recognize your limitations and then take action to remove them. Any limits you put on yourself are going to be infinitely more damaging than any limits that ever could be placed upon you by society or other external influences.

In this book you are going to learn the value of your mindset and what you can do to stop limiting yourself and open yourself up to achieving anything you desire. The more you work towards your personal development and working through these limitations, the further you are going to be able to go in terms of achieving your millionaire status.

Millionaires understand that their status is achieved by much more than just money. It involves a careful balance of personal development, self-discipline, and determination. Without these elements there is simply no way to become a millionaire. If you want to become a millionaire the first thing you must do is learn about all that goes into becoming one and then prepare yourself to become that person. When you live congruent with the way a true millionaire lives then you have the greatest opportunity to become a millionaire in your own life. Once you learn about all that goes into creating a millionaire you can start mirroring these habits and activities in your own life and then you will see major advancements towards you becoming a millionaire yourself.

Chapter 2: Millionaire Mindset

"I used to define success as being able to produce any results you wanted, whether it was a relationship, weight-loss, being a millionaire, impacting the culture, changing society, whatever it might be - it might be homelessness, whatever. Lately, I've redefined success as 'fulfilling your souls purpose'."

- Jack Canfield

Millionaires achieve their status by understanding the importance of mindset. If you ask any millionaire about their mindset patterns you will learn that they are very strict about how they think about life and the world around them. They do not allow for themselves to foster negative mindset habits because they recognize how damaging these can be towards their total success. If a millionaire wants to make millions, they must be primed in order to do so. They can prime themselves by mastering their mindset and recognizing the strength of their mind as a tool in leveraging them towards making the millions they desire.

If you want to become a millionaire you need to understand the importance of your mind and how your mindset patterns and behaviors can affect your success. Being able to succeed comes from great discipline, an ability to control your mind effectively, and high emotional intelligence. Not one millionaire features a low level of emotional intelligence. If they do, they will not retain their status for a long period of time and therefore they should not be considered an idol or role model.

There are many unique ways that millionaires use their mindset as a tool to achieve success. In order for you to achieve success you must understand and utilize these methods to achieve your success. The following mindset behaviors and patterns are ones that you need to embrace if you are going to become a millionaire. Give yourself adequate time to actually integrate each of these patterns into your life so that you can truly gain maximum benefit from them. Recognize that these need to be permanent lifestyle changes. If you treat these like a phase or a fad, you are not going to gain lasting benefits from them.

Live Within' Your Means

People who are rich recognize what it means to live within' their means and they do it. People who are wealthy do not get there by burning through their life savings and spending everything they have in life. Instead, they recognize their net worth and they live within' their means. Because of this type of modesty, they are able to increase their means rapidly over time. Even once a rich person becomes millionaire, multi-millionaire or billionaire, they will still look for good deals and bargains. Wealthy people almost never pay full-price for anything, and if they do it's because it is worth the investment. They are able to recognize the importance of money and they seek to spend it in the best possible methods.

Never Gamble

Wealthy people don't gamble. Did you know that 77% of people who struggle financially play the lottery on a regular basis? This is because they don't understand what actually goes into creating financial wealth and so they seek to make fast money this way. The truth is, they will probably never win it. Rich people like to know where their money is going and they value odds that are in their favor. Knowing how poorly the odds are stacked in the lottery means that it's a no-brainer that they won't gamble at all. It simply isn't worth it. Rich people want to invest in means that get results, not chance.

Read Daily

88% of wealthy people read for 30 minutes or more every single day. Reading offers you the opportunity to learn more, to engage in personal development, and to expand your mind. You can learn an infinite amount of knowledge through regular reading. If you want to be a millionaire, you should embrace reading. There is knowledge within' written text that you simply can't find anywhere else. Ideally, you should seek to read a book each week. The more you read, the better. Always set aside time for reading on a daily basis.

Spend Less Time in Front of Screens

People who spend their time in front of screens on a regular basis are not productive. There are statistics that show that two-thirds of all of the wealthy people in the world watch TV for less than an hour per day, alternatively 77% of those who are struggling financially spend an hour or more watching TV on a daily basis. 74% or more of those who are struggling financially spend one or more hour each day using the Internet recreationally. If you want to be a millionaire, you need to cut out the distractions that come with regular screen time. While there is nothing wrong with using the internet or watching TV, you need to be prepared to reduce your screen time so that you can invest your time into activities that will actually get you results.

Control Your Emotions

People who are incapable of controlling their emotions will struggle to reach success in life. A lack of control over your emotions can lead to you saying things you regret, making decisions you regret, and ultimately sabotaging your own ability to succeed in life. Instead of self-sabotaging in this way, learn to develop your emotional intelligence. The more you can identify and control your emotions, the easier it will be for you to master your mindset and establish healthy behaviors that will allow you to be more productive in life. Never let your emotions control you, learn to control your emotions.

Network and Volunteer on A Regular Basis

There is a great amount of value that comes from networking and volunteering on a regular basis. When you are engaged in activities only for the profit, people will begin to believe that you are not genuine. You will also struggle to become known or noticed by other people. If you want to become visible and recognized, you need to network and volunteer on a regular basis. This builds a positive reputation for yourself, and it also increases the amount of visibility you gain. You never know who you will meet when you attend regular events without the intention of making business deals and earning money.

Work Hard

Rich people don't get rich by being lazy and working minimal hours. If you want to be rich, you need to work hard. Wake up, show up, and stay as long as it takes to make each day a success. Those who wake up late, arrive late, and leave early in favor of having fun are never going to make a millionaire lifestyle. Instead, they are going to struggle with their finances forever. While it is important that you play hard when it is time for play, you should also be working hard when it is time to work. Make sure that you work twice as hard than you play so that when it comes time to play you can completely let loose and not worry that you are losing more money than you are earning during your leisure time.

Set Goals

A millionaire never works towards "something". They work towards "the thing". They never wing it: they set goals and they achieve them. There is no value in working towards an unidentified goal. You will never feel motivated to achieve it and therefore you will never achieve anything in life. Instead, you will go further backwards than you would have if you had simply set goals. Your goals should vary in size and length. You should have long-term goals that are going to serve you in the long run and you should have shorter goals that you can rapidly accomplish. Accomplishing shorter goals on a regular basis will give you the confidence and momentum you need to continue working towards the larger goals.

Never Procrastinate

Procrastinating is a habit that is fostered by those who do not achieve success in life. If you want to be successful, you need to ditch the habit of procrastination and work towards goals on a regular basis. Even the uncomfortable, unenjoyable and difficult tasks should be accomplished in a timely manner. If you procrastinate, you will never achieve what you need to in order to succeed at becoming a millionaire. Make a deal with yourself that any time you have a difficult or unenjoyable task that needs to be accomplished, you will do it first before any other tasks. That way, it is completely out of the way and you do not have to worry about it any longer. It will reduce stress, increase productivity, and leave you freedom in your schedule to accomplish anything you need to achieve.

Talk Less, Listen More

Nothing can be gained by spending too much time talking and not enough time listening. It is valuable to learn when it is a good time to talk and when you should be quiet and listen. Those who listen learn a great deal of information, gain perspective on life, and open up their opportunities. People love to be heard, so being able to listen effectively will allow people to feel heard and valued in life. This means that the important people who can contribute towards your success will enjoy talking to you. They will be more inclined to teach you, and help you achieve success in your life. You need to be coachable and you need to be willing to listen.

Avoid Toxic Relationships

Toxic relationships have a damaging effect on everyone involved. They can affect you in ways that will have devastating effects towards your ability to achieve success in life. If you want to be a success, you need to be willing to cut ties with toxic relationships and only welcome positive and productive relationships into your life. People who get caught in toxic relationships can rapidly deteriorate their feelings of self-worth, their self-esteem, and their self-confidence. They fail to achieve their goals because they begin to believe that their goals are not achievable. If you want to succeed, you need to stop having relationships with toxic people. Consider this: you are the sum of the five people you spend most of your time with. If you are spending time with level ones and twos, maybe even some level threes, you are never going to advance to level four or five wealth. You must be mindful over the people you spend your time with and spend time only with those who are as dedicated to success as you are.

Don't Give Up

You are going to hear "no" and other shut downs on a regular basis. This is true in life and in business. If you are not prepared to hear these rejections, you need to do whatever you can to prepare yourself. You are never going to get a straight-shot opportunity without any resistance, setbacks, defeats, mistakes, failures, or other obstacles that will hold you back for a period of time. If you want to be successful, you must be prepared to continue persevering towards your goals in spite of these resistances. Never give up, keep your goals in sight and always work towards them. The more you work towards your goals, the more likely you are going to achieve them. If you want to be a millionaire, you must never give up on your goals.

Ditch Limiting Beliefs

"I am not worthy", "I am not enough", "Success isn't for me", "I am not lucky", and other phrases are highly limiting in what they allow you to believe about yourself. If you constantly dumb yourself down for your beliefs, you are never going to achieve success in your life. You must be prepared to ditch your limiting beliefs and start thinking positive thoughts. Whenever a limiting belief enters your mind you should take the time to identify it and then eliminate it. When you do this effectively, you will be able to release the limiting beliefs and open up the opportunity for you to expand your options. You are only as small as you think you are. If you want to be bigger than you are, think bigger than you are. It is that simple.

Make Your Own Luck

People who wait for luck are people who play the lottery and expect to win it. It *may* happen, but the odds are not good enough to bet on. If you want to be a millionaire, you have to make your own luck. Develop positive habits, work on your personal development, recognize your negative behaviors and eliminate them, look for opportunities pursue bonuses, new businesses and good health, and do everything within' your control to advance yourself through life. There is no value in waiting for the luck of the draw to fall into your lap. If you want to succeed in life, you have to make your own luck and pave the way to your own success.

Know Your Purpose

It is important that you understand what your purpose is in life. People who pursue money believing that riches is their purpose are the same type of people who end up rich and devastated. If you want to enjoy your life, you must identify what your purpose is and work in alignment with your life's purpose. Pursue your lifelong dream and you will become the wealthier *and* happiest of the people in the world. However, pursue riches without any intention to discover or pursue your purpose and you will be one of the poorest in the world. If you don't know what your purpose is, your very first mission is to find out.

Adapt to Change

The final thing you need to master as a millionaire is your ability to adapt to change. Change happens all around us, and when you're involved with something as volatile as money you need to be able to adapt to change. There are going to be days where your money takes a major hit, and there are going to be days where it increases beyond your wildest dreams. There are going to be days when nothing goes the way you planned, and there are going to be days where everything goes perfectly. If you want to succeed in life you need to be prepared to adapt to the changes that are taking place around you. There is rarely anything you can do to control these changes, and it is not worth it to try. Instead, you need to understand that these changes are beyond your control and adapt the best way that you can. Seek out where advantages can be gained and use these to help advance you towards your success. If all else fails, practice your ability to accept defeat and mistakes.

Becoming a millionaire means mastering the millionaire mindset. Millionaires do not achieve this status by living with limiting beliefs, poor habits, and negative mindset and behaviors that do not serve their highest good. If you want to be a millionaire you need to recognize the value of your mindset behaviors and how they affect your long-term success. There is no other way to become a millionaire than to master yourself. The "secret" of being a millionaire is that wealth is acquired as a direct reflection of the amount of personal success you create in your life. The more you practice personal development, the greater your wealth will grow.

Chapter 3: Habits of Millionaires and Billionaires

"The probability of creating financial freedom depends on the system you are using."

- Mark Victor Hanson

Believe it or not, many millionaires have habits that you would not expect. As an average middle-income person, you likely have been taught to believe that millionaires are all about having the most expensive wardrobe, clothes, homes, and vacations. You likely have been lead to believe that they spend millions on luxurious things and that money just slips through their fingers like water through the faucet. The reality is, the opposite is true.

Millionaires do not become millionaires by spending like millionaires. Instead, they become millionaires by recognizing the value of money and respecting it in a way that allows them to maintain it and manage it effectively. Most millionaires boast about their ability to spend as little as possible. While they may be buying houses, cars, and other luxuries, you can almost certainly guarantee that they are shopping for every bargain possible along the way.

A millionaire gets to be a millionaire because they learn how to save money. They learn the value of money and they learn how to spend it in a way that maintains its value for them. The items they invest in are always high quality and almost always maintain their value even long after being purchased. If you want to be a millionaire, you need to learn to respect money in this same way. The following are five millionaire habits that you need to start practicing immediately.

Stay Positive

A positive mindset is invaluable to a millionaire. If you want to be a millionaire, you need to learn to have a positive mindset and stay that way as often as possible. Being positive doesn't mean that you don't experience negative emotions. It simply means that you know how to take those negative emotions and manage them effectively, and then turn everything around so that it is positive once again. If you want to be a millionaire, you must learn to look for the silver lining in every situation.

Hang Out with Other Successful People

Millionaires hang out with other millionaires. Those who don't earn the same amount as they do simply don't have the same mindset and therefore it is difficult for them to be around. If a millionaire were to spend a significant amount of time with non-millionaires, it is almost certain that they would lose their wealth. You should always seek to surround yourself with other successful people who are heading in the same direction as you are. Spending time with people who aren't will lead you backwards and will result in you not earning as much as you potentially could if you spent your time more wisely with a better choice of people.

Pursue Your Own Goals

People who are successful don't get there by investing their entire life in achieving other people's goals for them. They are not employees, they are employers. They want to be at the top because they know that is where the real income lies, and they will do anything to be there. If you are going to be a millionaire you need to learn to identify your own goals and then pursue them. Never let anyone or anything stand in your way, simply pursue them fearlessly and fiercely so that you can achieve success in your own life in a way that serves you.

Have A Mentor

Having a mentor is invaluable when you are seeking to become successful. They give you the opportunity to hop into the fast lane as they can give you advice and knowledge to help draw you forward in your business and in life. Having a successful mentor will help you by influencing your life in a positive way. By regularly checking in with your mentor and working together with them, you will always have motivation to move forward and achieve success in your life and business. This will help guarantee that you earn millions.

Respect Money

Not one single millionaire disrespects money. The only ones who do are the ones who come into large amounts unexpectedly and then rapidly lose it all due to having no respect for money. If you are going to be a millionaire and stay that way, you need to learn about the value of money and respect it in a way that will enable you to maintain and manage your money effectively. You need to understand the value of a dollar and always respect that value.

Be Willing to Make Sacrifices

People who become wealthy must learn to make sacrifices. There are many things you must sacrifice in life in order to become wealthy. In fact, this is one of the primary reasons why people believe wealth is the root of all evil. An untrained millionaire or billionaire will give up all of the most important things in life to become wealthy. While they will certainly be able to generate their wealth, they will never be able to enjoy it, or their life. If you want to be a successful millionaire, you must learn what to sacrifice and when. For example, sacrifice party time and entertainment time to work, not your family time, though. Your family, the people who love you, and the people you love are important. If you need to free up more time so that you can generate your wealth, free it up by sacrificing the time you spend doing extra things like partying, watching TV, and relaxing.

You must also be willing to sacrifice your original dream. As you evolve, the dream you have is going to change and therefore what you are working towards will also evolve. You need to be willing to accept that and adjust your vision and your goals while you work towards success in your life.

Be an Entrepreneur

You will soon learn the differences between types of income, but for now you need to understand the primary method of obtaining income that you need to understand. Linear income, or income you get directly for the work you do, should never be obtained through a government job, nor through being someone else's employee. Regardless of what level of financial security that may provide you with, it will also provide you with financial chains. You will never be in control; therefore, you will never be able to inflate the income you earn through your linear source. You must be willing to be an entrepreneur if you are going to generate enough income to become a millionaire or billionaire. Without being your own boss, you will put a ceiling on your success and you will never surpass what your company is willing to let you grow to.

No Excuses

Millionaires and billionaires never make excuses. Whether they are tired, bored, unhappy with the task at hand, would rather be having fun, or anything else, they will never make an excuse. They understand that work must be done, and they are willing to do it so that they can earn an income. Without their willingness to work with no excuses, they will never earn enough of an income to become a millionaire, much less a billionaire. Putting things off, procrastinating, and using excuses instead of earning results are all habits of people who will never generate wealth in their life.

Get Quality Sleep

You must be able to have the energy to work each day, so getting quality sleep is important. Not every millionaire or billionaire sleeps for a full eight hours each night, but each one certainly makes sure that he or she is getting quality sleep each time they rest their eyes. Without quality sleep, you will never have the energy you need to keep going on a daily basis. Millionaires often have full schedules, and they must be able to maintain these schedules if they are going to maintain their wealth. If you cannot commit to this all due to a lack of energy then you will lose your wealth, if you even gain it in the first place. You must always commit to a quality rest every single night.

Write Down 10 Ideas Every Day

The ideas you have on a regular basis are important. Creativity serves your entrepreneurship and therefore you must always encourage yourself to stay creative. It can be highly beneficial to get into the habit of writing down 10 ideas every single day. While not all of these ideas will be useable or beneficial, they will keep you working towards generating new ideas. Every so often, you will come across an idea you come up with that may be another million-dollar-idea. When you do, put it into action and go earn your million!

Learn to Say No

Just because opportunities present themselves doesn't mean you have to say yes. Being a slave to the word "yes" can keep you poor. You must learn how to schedule yourself by recognizing what activities are beneficial and worthwhile and which ones aren't. If you stretch yourself too thin, you are going to end up spending your energy on things that aren't beneficial and your financial wealth will suffer as a result. Additionally, if something does not serve you or make you happy, you should not pursue it. It is absolutely okay to say no to things that are not beneficial to your overall situation. These things are typically, in fact, the opposite of beneficial and can drain your valuable energy and leave you feeling unhappy and frustrated during precious time that should be spent focusing on how you can increase your wealth. Learn to say no.

Plant Seeds Everywhere

True people of wealth know that there are opportunities everywhere. As a result, they are always planting seeds so that they can take advantage of opportunities and increase their likelihood of generating wealth in various areas. You should always take the time to plant seeds everywhere you. When you are networking, when you are faced with favorable business opportunities, when you have new ideas, and whenever anything else comes up that may benefit your wealth in one way or another, always plant a seed. This doesn't necessarily mean that you will see to it that each seed will flourish, but it gives you the opportunity to get on board with nearly anything that shows complete promise, instead of being left out of the loop because you didn't take the time to plant seeds.

Stand Next to The Smartest Person in The Room

There are many benefits that can come from standing next to the smartest person in the room. When you do, you are seen as a smart person as well, and you instantly gain some level of social status simply by your placement in the room. As well, you gain the opportunity to talk to them and ask questions so that you can learn more about what they are knowledgeable in. Finally, it also gives you the opportunity to network and get yourself "in" with smarter people. Smarter people are generally wealthier people, so when you are "in" with these people, you gain the ability to increase your own status and wealth exponentially just based on these connections alone.

Maintain Your Health

No one ever got rich by lying in a hospital bed because they failed to maintain their health. If you want to be rich, you must maintain your health. The healthier you are, the more you will be able to stay on your feet and continue pursuing your wealth and riches. You must learn how you can maintain your health in a way that prevents you from getting sick and serves you by providing you with greater energy. Always eat properly, and foster a workout plan that will allow you to stay physically active. The more you maintain your health, the more wealth you will be able to generate for yourself.

Do The Stuff You Love Each Day

Wealthy people understand the value of life and that not every minute of the day should be spent doing work-related tasks. In fact, wealthy people love to have fun. You should make time every single day to do at least one thing that you genuinely love doing. Furthermore, try doing stuff you loved doing as a kid as these are typically the purest passions that you carry. Paint, ride a bike, hike, read comic books, do anything that makes your heart happy. This will all contribute to the quality of your life, which is important when you want to generate wealth.

Follow Up with People

Whether it's for business or in personal life, you should always follow up with people. Follow up with clients to let them know you've been thinking about them and to see if they are enjoying their purchases, follow up with employees to see if they are pleased with their jobs, and follow up with suppliers and other businesses you work with to see how they are feeling about your business interactions. As well, follow up with friends, family, and anyone else of importance to see how they are doing in life. The more you follow up with people, the better. Personal connections are important when you are building an empire, as no empire was ever built alone. You should always invest time in nurturing your connections with people both inside and outside of your business.

Be Bold

While you don't need to reinvent the wheel, you can certainly benefit from spinning it in a unique way. In business and in life, you need to learn to be bold and be brave. Take the actions that no one else is taking, make bold moves that come with risks, and move yourself and your company towards major success by ditching the "shy guy" act. It is never beneficial to be shy or timid in a setting where you want to generate success. Always be willing to be bold and be brave. Talk to the people who seem "out of your league", take major steps towards change, and lift yourself up towards being incredible.

Never Be in A Rush

If you find that you are rushing, you are not managing yourself and your schedule correctly. You should never be in a rush. Being in a rush leaves lose ends and it leads to sloppiness. If you want to be a millionaire or a billionaire, you must learn to manage yourself and your schedule appropriately and never be in a rush. Always schedule plenty of time for each task to be completed. Millionaires and billionaires who are in a rush are always at risk of losing everything, that is why they are rushing. They also end up deteriorating their health and so their financial wealth suffers regardless. Don't let that be you.

Learn to Communicate

Millionaires know how to communicate, and they can communicate effectively. They know how to listen, they know when to speak, and they know what to say. They are always one step ahead of the rest of the conversation, so they are incredible at guiding it in any direction they desire. Wealthy people are extremely smart, and they know exactly how to use communication as one of their most powerful tools. Since communication is one of the primary methods of acquiring wealthy by getting what you want and what you need, you must learn how to communicate effectively and efficiently with those around you. Start small, and work your way up. Eventually, you will be able to communicate with anyone you desire to achieve any outcome you desire.

If you want to be a millionaire or a billionaire, you must learn to foster the habits of one. The more you learn to take on these habits and apply them into your own life, the more success you are going to generate towards your goals. Being able to act like a millionaire now, before you even have wealth, will give you the best opportunity to become a millionaire in the near future. Start acting as though you have money in the bank now, and you will see that very soon the money truly will be in your bank account. It is not the law of attraction; it is the law of life.

Chapter 4: You Must Be Better Than Everyone

"Conquer your challenges by accepting the fact that you must be greater than any challenge (or person) that comes your way."

-   Alex Becker

Only 1% of the population is rich, and in order for you to be a part of that 1% you must be better than absolutely everyone else. There is no room to be great and there is no room to be awesome, you must be incredible, period. If you want to be rich, you must learn to be better than every single other person in the room, or you won't be rich and it's that simple.

If you were to fill a room with 100 people and look at them 40 years down the line, only 1 of those 100 people would be rich. The chances of becoming rich are incredibly slim, and the only possible opportunity for you to become rich is to settle for nothing less. You must understand that the millionaire mindset leaves no wiggle room to be anything less than absolutely impeccable. You must be the absolute best at everything you do by being better than everyone else who is doing it.

Of course, you are not going to be the best right off the bat. It is going to take you time to learn how to do things, and it is going to take you time to learn how to do them well. But, if you want to be a millionaire, you must be dedicated to learning. You must be absolutely committed to the fact that you are going to be better than everyone else and you will do absolutely everything within' your power to see to it that you are. If you are not willing to commit to this level, you will never succeed as a millionaire.

People who are not willing to be better than everyone else do not end up rich. They end up a part of the middle class, or lower. At best, they may end up a part of the upper-middle class. But, I am guessing that you aren't here to learn how to be any level of middle-class. Instead, you want to learn how you can be a part of the elite upper-class society that is filled only with those who are brilliant enough to earn themselves the wealth they desire.

Being better than everyone else can be uncomfortable. You are going to run into situations where you are going to have to be willing to admit that you are better than others. You might lose friends and loved ones because they simply can't handle admitting that you have done better than they have. You might end up surrounded by people who are all striving to be better than the rest and therefore you are not always the best in the room. The point is that you are going to be uncomfortable. You must always be willing to work to be better than everyone else in the room so that you can comfortably sail into riches. Even when you are surrounded by people who possess more wealth than yourself, you must be willing to strive to be the best in the room. It may not happen that exact minute, but work to make it happen in the very near future.

It is very important to understand that part of being better than everyone else in the room is being confident in that knowledge. If you spend your entire time in the room showing off how much better you are, you are not going to be effective at advancing yourself to greater wealth. You will rapidly shut down your ability to communicate, listen, and learn, and therefore you will never get past where you are. You must always strive to do better than you are today, which means you must always be willing to communicate effectively, listen, and learn. Being arrogant will never lead you towards success, nor wealth.

People who are wealthy and who are better than others in the room are confident in this. They do not need to rub it into the faces of others. In fact, if asked they are almost always more than willing to share and work to help others be better as well. They never take the time to show off how much better they are by making others feel poorly. Those who do are often not as wealthy as one might think, as they are frequently making up for it by talking a big talk without having anything to back it up.

To be truly wealthy, you must understand the important balance of being better than everyone else in the room and being comfortable with that knowledge. You must learn to find comfort in the discomfort of losing friends and family and of being treated as though you are different from everyone else. After all, you *are* different when you are a part of 1% of the entire population.

You cannot erase the fact that not everyone will be able to relate to you because not everyone will be experiencing what you are experiencing. Not everyone will understand what it is like to be a part of that 1%, and that is the beauty of it. If they could understand, then there would be no 1% because everyone would be wealthy and wealth would be of little to no importance. If you want to be truly wealthy, you must learn to come to terms with this now. Only then will you be able to truly embrace the wealthy lifestyle and lead yourself into being a millionaire. So, are you willing to admit that you are destined to be better than everyone else that you know?

Chapter 5: Types of Income

"The moment you make passive income and portfolio income a part of your life, your life will change. Those words will become flesh."

-   Robert Kiyosaki

There are two types of income that millionaires and billionaires use to generate their wealth. These two are the primary types that are responsible for their ability to create enough wealth that they can do virtually anything they desire. The two types are: linear income and passive income.

Linear Income

Linear income is a very basic sense of income. It is the money you get for the work you do, whether it be a career title you hold or a job you have done for someone else. Linear income is an important source of income for virtually anyone, and even the richest people on earth continue to utilize linear income as an opportunity to generate wealth. However, linear income should not be relied on alone. Those who rely solely on linear income will always be a slave to their career or job, because without it they will no longer carry any wealth-making opportunities. In addition to your linear income, you want to add various forms of passive income.

Passive Income

Passive income is a mandatory part of generating and maintaining millionaire status. People who want to become millionaires learn the value of passive income and how to master it. Passive income is the type of income that you earn when you sleep. If you'll recall the levels of wealth, level five comprises of the level of people who generate money while they are sleeping.

There are infinite numbers of passive income stream you can acquire, but millionaires only engage in the ones that will actually make an impact on their income levels. If you want to increase the amount of income you are earning, then the following seven types of passive income are important for you to explore. These options will allow you to earn an income while you sleep, assisting you with moving towards everything you need to be to be a true millionaire.

Earning a passive income allows you to make money effortlessly. It increases the quality of your life by giving you the opportunity to live comfortably. You stop having to work so hard for your income and you start being able to work in ways that are more effective and productive. You give yourself a cushion to make mistakes or claim defeat, which is important when you are leading a millionaire lifestyle.

Method #1: Selling Evergreen Products

Evergreen products are any product that can stand alone without you having to do anything extra when you make the sale. Live courses or events and programs require you to actually put in work in return for the income you are gaining. However, say you were to write a book, launch a self-paced course, or sell a video with important information for certain people. This type of product has already been completed, so all of the sales you are making come from effective marketing plans. You do not have to do any additional work for the income you are receiving, you are completely done by this point.

Evergreen products are a powerful way to sell and earn income while you are sleeping. By taking your knowledge you can put together a stand-alone product, have a landing page made for your sales, market the product and sell it. You can either do all of the work of marketing, or you can outsource this part and hiring a marketing manager to cover this part of your business. Then, you simply earn all of the profits from the sales.

Method #2: Real Estate Investments

Real estate investments are an option for people who have a higher income, and they have a high amount of potential. When you get into real estate, there are many ways that you can earn money and increase your income. Rental properties, vacation rentals, and flipping houses are all excellent opportunities to invest in real estate and make money back.

If you want to build your income through rental properties and vacation rentals, you will need to get some money behind you so that you can actually purchase these properties. Once you have, you can get renters into each property and start profiting! Rental properties are an excellent long-term investment because you gain a small amount of profit up front, once the property is paid off you get significantly more each month from rental fees, and whenever you decide to you can sell the property and earn a large income from it.

Flipping houses is another great way to make money from real estate. You can invest in foreclosed properties or inexpensive fixer-uppers and then fix the place up and flip it. There are many tips, ideas, and rules around flipping houses that will make it a successful source of income for you. If you choose to get into flipping houses you should take some time to research this option and how it works to ensure that you maximize your profits from this venture.

Nearly everyone who has a large sum of money is invested in real estate in one way or another. Real estate is something that will always be profitable as people are always going to need houses. If you want to invest in real estate, you will almost certainly get your money back plus more every single time.

Method #3: Outsource Work

One way to turn earned income into passive income is to outsource the work you are doing. For example, if you are building a business you can start outsourcing various parts of your work, eventually outsourcing the entire thing so that you can focus your attention elsewhere on earning income through a new or alternative means.

Outsourcing can be done in many ways, you can hire new sales employees, assistants, marketing teams, and virtually any other number of employees to run your business. The more employees you hire, the more passive your income will become. It is crucial that you always make sure that you are hiring the right people for your team, however, as hiring the wrong ones can result in you losing income. It is not beneficial to have someone in a position if they are not capable of producing the results you are looking for.

Method #4: Investment Portfolios

Having a rich investment portfolio can work to your favor when it comes to increasing your income. There are many different ways that you can invest, from investing in stocks, to investing in mutual funds and other methods. You can invest on your own with your own knowledge, but ideally you should work together with an investment broker to help you. Financial advisors and investment brokers are highly trained with turning investments into greater income, so they can help you make the right decisions to ensure that you earn maximum profit from your investments.

One thing you should note is that a rich investment portfolio is one that is highly diversified. You want to be able to recognize this and invest in as many different positive areas as possible. The more you invest, the more likely you are going to be able to increase the amount of profit you are making. It also helps mitigate risk and prevent you from losing large amounts of money.

Method #5: Royalty Income

Earning royalty income is an excellent opportunity to earn a passive income. Royalties are gained by taking part in someone else's project and then earning royalties as a result of your involvement. Aside from your involvement in creating the project, you do not have to do anything in regards to maintaining it, marketing it, or otherwise building the project. All you must do is uphold your part of the deal and then the rest falls into place.

If you play your cards right, royalties can pay you a large amount of money. You can earn money on an ongoing basis for a long period of time as long as you invest your time into projects that are certain to be a success. Always make sure to learn as much as you can about the project beforehand, and then assuming it is a positive investment of your time, go ahead and invest. That will lead you to successfully receiving royalty income on work you have done.

Method #6: Startup Investments

Once you have enough money to invest, it is a good idea to consider investing in startup businesses. The average silent investor or angel investor must be able to invest at least $100,000 into startups in order to be involved, but once you can reach this point it is a great opportunity to increase your net worth rapidly.

Before you start investing in startup businesses you should take the time to research what goes into making a successful startup. Take some time to learn from other investors and understand how you can invest your money in a way that mitigates your risk and ensures that you have the highest chance of gaining your money back. When you do this, you ensure that you are knowledgeable enough to turn these investments into a valuable income stream. If you do not want to start investing in startups on your own, you may consider going in with a partner or a small team of investors in the beginning. Doing this can help you learn the ropes and can keep you from risking too much of your money into startups before you are fully knowledgeable in how to invest in the right ones.

Method #7: Franchising

Another wonderful way to earn passive income is to franchise your business. If you have a type of business that can be franchised, franchising it can earn you a large passive income. With franchises, you will earn money from each new chain that is opened up. As a result, you will earn money from other people starting their own businesses underneath you.

Franchising can be a bit difficult at first and it can take some thoughtful planning to get started, but once your business is up and running you can begin earning major profit from this business model. If you do not currently have a business that can be franchised, you should consider starting up a business that can later be franchised. Work on building up the initial business and once it's large enough you can invest in the process of turning it into a franchise. Then you can reap in all of the benefits of being the primary owner of a franchise chain.

Passive income provides you with a powerful opportunity to enjoy true financial security. This is not the type of financial security that involves you having a guaranteed paycheck at the end of each pay period from your employer. Instead, it means that you are literally earning money while you sleep and that you are earning even more when you actually try. When you are able to earn passive income in this way, you open yourself up to experience true financial freedom. You can begin doing anything you desire because you know that you will have a steady stream of income coming your way regardless of what you are doing. Of course, if you want to be a millionaire and stay one, you will be spending your time invested in the next major business venture you will be pursuing. Remember, level five wealth involves you making money while you sleep, and passive income is the key for you to do that.

Chapter 6: Take Advantage of the Internet

The internet has produced more millionaires in recent times than nearly any other business platform. It is no secret that in this day and age, the internet is a valuable resource that can help you accomplish virtually anything you set out to achieve. If you want to be a millionaire, you need to embrace the internet, take advantage of it, and learn to leverage it as an income-producing opportunity.

There are many ways to use the internet to your advantage. It starts with understanding the way the internet can be used and identifying ways that you can personally use it to generate revenue. Following that, you can begin building up your foundation and launching your new income-producing method. You should use the internet to establish at least one of your income sources. The following are five ideas of how you can start earning an income online and turning it into either a passive or linear income stream.

YouTube Star

YouTube is popping out stars left, right and center and there is nothing to say you can't be one of them! YouTube has the potential to help earn you several thousands of dollars through filming, which you can do from any high quality video camera. There are YouTube channels about virtually any topic you can think of. You can find channels with entertainers who provide comedy for viewers, you can find business-oriented channels who teach you about marketing and running a business, you can find channels that teach you about various hobbies and skills. There are limitless topics for what YouTube channels can feature.

If you want to take advantage of YouTube and start earning an income through filming yourself, you can get started extremely easy. All you need is a high quality camera and a creative imagination. Think about something you are passionate about as well as knowledgeable in and start filming about it! You can teach, entertain, or even simply share. There are many vloggers out there who share day-to-day information about their lives and make money doing it! All you need is the desire to make money and the ability to use a camera and upload your films to YouTube. From there, you monetize your videos, do some basic marketing and viola you have a successful YouTube channel!

There are many YouTube stars who are earning enough to purchase homes, cars, and anything else they desire. They are able to turn their YouTube channel into their full-time income and as a result they can do anything they want, so long as they are filming on a regular basis. If you want to take advantage of online income resources, YouTube is a great place to start.

Online Retailer

If you are not as camera savvy, you might consider an alternative such as opening up an online retail shop. Online retailers make thousands of dollars each year, and the amount of growth you can sustain is limitless. The best income-producing online retail model is to start a dropshipping company. This way, you do not have to pay a significant amount of money to obtain inventory and ship it to your customers. Instead, all inventory and shipping-related tasks are managed by your wholesaler. All you have to do is run the website, plug in products, and market your page! You can even outsource the website maintenance and marketing positions to other people who want to produce an income online so that your online retailer income is entirely passive.

Online retailers have many advantages to being able to plug into the market. You have a global market right off the bat, meaning you can target any segment of the market and reach a significantly higher number of your audience than you would if you had a physical store front that you were trying to promote. The overhead and startup fees are a fraction of what it costs to start a brick and mortar business, and you can do nearly anything you desire with your business. Simply look at Amazon.com: they started as an online bookstore and have since expanded into selling virtually everything you can think of. They are now an online marketplace for various retailers and as a result of their ingenious platform they have been able to create a multi-billion-dollar company that is leading the online retail industry.

Blogger

Believe it or not, bloggers are still relevant in the online space and still have the potential to make a large amount of money online. Many people assume that blogging is on its way out, but there are several blogs that are doing better than ever. The reality is that blogs make up a large part of the online space. Many people rely on blogs for research purposes, specifically in traveling, lifestyle, and consumerism situations. When people are looking to take a trip or purchase a new item, for example, they will often refer to their favorite online blogs to discover which ones are the best investments. Likewise, if someone is looking to decorate their house, purchase a new wardrobe, or otherwise make a significant change in their lifestyle, they will often consult a blog to see where the current trends are heading so that they can remain trendy.

Blogging is relatively simple and it doesn't take much to start. Simply use a platform like WordPress or Blogger and start typing away! With some marketing and monetization, you will be able to turn your blog into an income-earning resource in no time. It is a great way to earn a blog while tapping into your market and increasing the amount of value you have to offer existing clients. Blogging is often considered to be an excellent addition to any online or offline business.

Affiliate Marketing

If you want to take things a step further, you should consider affiliate marketing. This is not necessarily network marketing, although network marketing can earn you a large amount as well, but affiliate marketing is the process where you work together with companies to promote their products. In return, they pay you a commission off of each sale you make for them.

Turning affiliate marketing into an income-producing activity is simple. As long as you have an online presence, you can become a successful affiliate marketer. The more online presences you have on various platforms, the more income you are going to be able to produce through affiliate marketing. You can promote your affiliate links on YouTube, blogs, social media platforms, and even in the offline space when you are chatting with friends and family. There are many companies that offer affiliate programs, including smaller indie businesses and larger ones like Amazon.com. You can take advantage of these platforms to help boost your income in general, or use it as a sidekick towards any other online-income-producing activity so that you can increase the amount of income you are generating in the online space.

Design an App

There is an app for nearly everything these days, and for a very good reason. Apps are a wonderful tool to use on smart phones, computers, tablets, and other mobile devices that people are constantly plugged into. They provide convenience, resources, entertainment, and other valuable assets to people's mobile devices. Using apps can make your mobile device a more customized version of what you need and want when you are carrying it around with you.

Designing an app and promoting it can give you the opportunity to earn passive income online. If you produce a high quality app and sell it you can earn between $0.99 and $14.99 per download, with the average resting between $1.99 and $4.99. With a proper marketing strategy in place you can earn as much or as little as you want through selling your app, all based on how much effort you are putting into the marketing strategy. A wonderful thing about apps is that you can simply update your app and market it all over again as a newer, updated version of the app that people have grown to know and love. This keeps your market fresh and maintains the lifespan of your app to be one that is longer than any other product that may simply be promoted and then die out once the initial version has been consumed by the target audience.

There are many other ways to take advantage of the internet to produce income, but these are certainly the most accessible ones to the average person. If you want to become a millionaire, it is important that you don't overlook the value of online business.

Tapping into this wealthy resource can give you the opportunity to earn a significantly higher amount of income through little to no effort. A wonderful thing about online companies is that you can hire virtual assistants and the business will be completely run for you, making the income stream extremely passive. There are many opportunities to profit from the online space, even if you are not highly skilled with the internet and computers. It seriously pays to take advantage of the income opportunities that are made available by the internet.

Chapter 7: The Power of Your Team

"Ultimately, leadership is not about glorious crowning acts. It's about keeping your team focused on a goal and motivated to do their best to achieve it, especially when the stakes are high and the consequences really matter. It is about laying the groundwork for others' success, and then standing back and letting them shine."

- Chris Hadfield

No one became a millionaire by themselves, not even a lottery winner. Lottery winners win because everyone who plays has faith that someone will win and therefore they all throw in a couple of bucks and in the end someone wins it. Self-made millionaires get there because they know the value of their team and they invest in their team, therefore their team invests in them and they end up millionaires.

If you want to be a millionaire, you must understand the power of your team. You must always work towards making your team more powerful, and every decision you make should be for the benefit of your team.

Pick an Experienced Team

Before you start picking who your team members are going to be, you need to understand the importance of having an experienced team. Just because you are not completely experienced in every field doesn't mean that your team shouldn't be. Establishing a highly experienced team can give you the advantage of having knowledge on your side. Just because you don't always know what you're doing doesn't mean no one else should. A team that has been through the experience before and knows how to create success can draw you forward into success much more rapidly than you could by yourself, or with a team who was under qualified.

When you are building your team, consider each aspect of your business and life and build your team accordingly. Pick people who are going to be a major asset to your company and life. If you are paying them a salary, always invest in the highest experienced worker you can afford. More often than not, this investment will pay off big time in the long run when they help launch you forward into major success.

Think of your team as your empire. You cannot create an empire by yourself, and you cannot create a monumental empire with a community of under qualified people who do not care to work together towards a common goal. It is vital that you work towards the common goal as an experienced unit, with each person being proficient in their respective area of business. This way, you can all rely on one another to successfully complete his or her part of the job and you can expect that success will come as a result.

Creating the Perfect Team

Picking your team can be a daunting task, but it is also the most important one. Before you hire anyone or choose anyone to play on your team, you need to understand the five primary points of picking people for your team. Being able to recognize these and use them to your advantage will ensure that you are building a team that is qualified and that will bring you forward into success.

Always Identify Weak Spots

Before you start hiring anyone to be a part of your team, identify your weak spots. You should also identify your strengths. Ideally, you want to hire people whose strengths are your weaknesses. That way, you each have a unique duty to fulfill that will bring you forward in your business.

Another way you should identify weaknesses is to recognize the strengths and weaknesses in other people. In doing so, you will be able to hire additional team members that will complement the existing team you have already created. You want to make sure that the entire team is created mindfully so that they all work together in a way that will ensure your success. If you have members who clash or who do not work together well, you are going to end up compromising your success.

Identify Your Time Commitments

In the beginning, you will want to be modest about how many people you are hiring. Consider what your time commitments are, and understand how much time you need each position to devote to their job. It is important to recognize how often you are going to need certain jobs completed in order for your entire team to work productively. Once you recognize this, you can hire part- and full-time employees to fill each respective position. It is also important, however, that you recognize the value of a good employee. If you find someone who is completely qualified but can only work part-time instead of full-time, you might consider hiring them and hiring an additional part-time worker to make up for the remaining time. Valuable employees who can become a major asset to your team should never be overlooked unless you absolutely have to.

Discover Potential Candidates

Take some time to truly identify who your potential candidates are. Right off the bat, you might recognize that some people are ill fit for the job. However, once it comes to picking the exact person, you want to really become critical over who you are picking. The final choice should be someone who compliments your team, works well with your existing staff, and can help draw you forward in your business. They should be a true asset to your team.

Take the time to look through each person's application, consider their interview, and weigh their strengths and weaknesses. Are they going to be reliable and capable of fulfilling the position you are seeking to fill? Will they be able to help you in important parts of business, or are they going to fall flat and leave you hanging? It is crucial that you pick members who are reliable and who will be dedicated to your success, recognizing that your success will also equal success for themselves.

Have Conversations

If you know someone who would fit perfectly on your team, it is not always necessary for you to have a formal interview. Instead, sit them down and have a conversation with them. Let them know about your business and your opportunity and extend a formal offer to them. This will give them the opportunity to learn about what you are doing and become a part of your team if they desire.

Always make sure that you keep this conversation formal enough to be about business, but not too formal. When you are working with people you already know, they generally won't want to be treated like you are a complete boss over them. Understand the value they can add and always stay personable with them. If you are not careful, you may end up pulling a power trip and losing a good friend, as well as the involvement of a valuable employee.

Hire The Right People and Pay Them Well

If you want to have the absolute best team, you need to be willing to hire the best people. The best people for your team are the ones that are good at what you aren't. If you are amazing at communicating but are not excellent at researching, you need to hire an amazing researcher. If you are amazing at executing plans but terrible at creating them, you need to hire an amazing planner. When you hire people who excel at your weaknesses, you build an indestructible team that will lead you towards absolute greatness.

In addition to hiring the best people, you need to pay them the best wages. If you do not take care of your own, they will not take care of you in return. Instead, they will eventually head off towards someone else who is willing to treat them better. When you get the right people on your team, you must do everything within' your power to keep them on your team. This includes paying them what they deserve to be paid, which is an amazing wage to match their amazing talent.

Constantly Assess Your Team

Just because your team has been built doesn't mean that you are done. You should constantly be assessing your team for opportunities to strengthen it. You always want to know where your strengths and weaknesses are, as this is what will give you the information you need to succeed. Knowing where your weaknesses are gives you the potential to hire new staff or make required changes to make sure that these weaknesses are being offset by talented staff.

You should have a system in place where you assess your staff on a regular basis. Take the time to consider where they are at and what type of asset they are providing your business with. If they are not proving to be an asset to your team, find a way to give them the opportunity to increase their productivity, or consider letting them go in favor of someone else who will do a better job.

Your team, whether it is in business or in life, is a vital part of you being able to succeed. If you want to succeed in life and in business, you need to be able to have a team behind you who knows how to work together in order to produce success. You should be able to trust that your team is going to work towards common goals and help bring you forward at every chance they get. If you do not have a strong team in place, or if you don't have a team at all, it is important that you put one together. A strong team will give you the assets, value, and knowledge that you need in order to become a millionaire. Not one single millionaire got there without the help of a team, and you won't either.

Chapter 8: Take The Pledge

"You're the driver of your own life, don't let anyone steal your seat."

- Unknown

If you have managed to stay committed to this book and read until now, then it is almost certain that you are ready to become a millionaire. Becoming a millionaire requires work, perseverance, determination, focus, and a willingness to succeed. If you think you have what it takes, then it is time for you to take the millionaire pledge.

The millionaire pledge is simple, but it is serious. In order for you to become a millionaire, you must be able to commit to this pledge. Without it, you will not have the commitment that you need in order to see your goal through. Let this be your first lesson in effective goal planning.

The pledge is simple for you to complete. You simply take a blank piece of paper, and write down the following:

"I, (insert your name), vow that I will do whatever it takes for me to become a millionaire. I recognize that it will take a lot of hard work, determination, and perseverance, and I commit to devoting myself to this goal. I will do whatever it takes to ensure that I reach this goal successfully. I recognize that there will be difficult times, and that there will be points where I must admit defeat and accept my mistakes. I am prepared to work towards the achievement of my goal knowing that these inevitable circumstances will arise, perhaps many times over. I commit to seeing myself through this goal and earning one million dollars, and from there earning several more. I will not stop until I become a millionaire."

Once you have written this down, or your own personalized variation of it, sign the paper, date it, and place it somewhere that you can see it on a daily basis. By physically seeing your commitment written down on a regular basis, you will be able to stay true to it and you will significantly increase your chances of achieving it. Affirming your goal on a daily basis is a great way to keep it fresh in your mind and stay motivated towards achieving it.

It is important that you make the process of witnessing your pledge a ritual that will work with you towards your success. Give yourself the opportunity to truly feel motivated and inspired by the pledge, and vow that you will always allow it to infuse your mind with positive thoughts when you are looking at it. You should never look at your pledge with a negative perspective or with the belief that you will not achieve it. If you do, you must rewrite the pledge and start over. Never tarnish your dream with thoughts of disbelief.

Conclusion

Becoming a millionaire is not as difficult as everyone thinks. There is a specific formula behind creating your millionaire status that can be achieved by virtually anyone. The only reason why more people are not millionaires is because they refuse to do the mindset work that will allow them to liberate themselves from limiting beliefs.

If you want to become a millionaire, you must be prepared to put in the work and effort that is required to become one. You cannot simply become a millionaire overnight. Anyone who does will almost certainly lose their wealth as they will not have the knowledge or discipline to maintain it. The mindset work is vital if you are going to become a millionaire and stay one.

This manual has given you every piece of information and advice that you need in order to become a millionaire. You have started by understanding what goes into creating a millionaire, the various levels of wealth, and the many habits and characteristics of millionaires. You have been given inspiration and advice on ways to begin creating your wealth, and you have been told of the importance of the various methods of building your wealth. Finally, you were instructed to take a pledge that required you to commit to your own success and achieve it. If you have reached this point, then there is no doubt that you have what it takes to become a millionaire.

I hope that this manual was informative and able to offer you valuable insight towards achieving your goals and becoming a millionaire. There is more that goes into being a millionaire than you likely realized, and understanding that is the first step of altering your life so that you can live congruent with what it truly means to be a millionaire.

There are many different factors that go into being a millionaire, but the key is that each millionaire recognizes the importance of their mind, body, and soul, and how each works together to create your most powerful tool: you. Once you learn about these unique parts of you and you learn to nurture and care for them effectively, you will be able to achieve any goal you set out to accomplish, including becoming a millionaire.

The next step is for you to start putting this advice into action. You need to begin structuring passive and linear income streams, and building your wealth in an effective manner that is going to keep it coming for a long time. You need to learn how you can view money with a more positive mindset, and you need to start building positive habits in your life. Once you have, you will start seeing positive and effective results in the way of your success.

Lastly, if you enjoyed this book I ask that you please take the time to review it on Amazon Kindle. Your honest feedback would be greatly appreciated.

Thanks and best of luck on the road to financial freedom and becoming a millionaire!